High Strange: United States Black Sites
Roswell to Area 51

To chart the black sites of the Unknown Fields city the studio commandeers an old US school bus and heads off on a reconnaissance trip from Roswell to Area 51, chronicling a series of aerial encounters from the borderlands of military outposts and the crater-pocked, fenced-off folkloric landscapes of the United States. The militarised landscapes which defend the city are hidden behind barbed wire, within inhospitable terrain or beneath the low resolution distortions of doctored satellite images. These concealed territories are our city walls and fortifications. But beyond their physical might, they are sites of psychological warfare, where rumour begins. Rumbling along UFO highways, past the mythic ground of Area 51, we explore territories of negotiation and conflict, zones of transgression, suspicion and speculation. Here as tall tales of conspiracy theorists and alien abductees mix with sonic booms crackling in the quiet desert air, we examine the mysteries and conspiracies that surround what lies off the map, off-grid and below the radar, proposing new truths and exposing alternative fictions.

High Strange is a graphic novel developed in response to the material Unknown Fields collected and the text written along this journey. All dialogue is taken from real interviews conducted with whistle-blowers, UFO researchers, local characters and military personnel. Collaged material is gathered en-route from declassified dossiers, alien enthusiast book stores, roadside gift shops and new age media. Unknown Fields embedded graphic novelist Kristian Donaldson operates on tour like a court room illustrator to visualise the conversations, sightings and first-hand accounts from the field. *High Strange* is a new conspiracy theory, stitched together from the stories unearthed in the shadowlands of the United States. It is a portrait of a landscape as a factory of fictions. A form of weaponised folklore. A territory that can be only understood by examining the stories the world tells about it.

IT DOES NOT SEEM THAT THE GOVERNMENT HAS ANY GAME PROGRAM IN PROGRESS FOR THE IDENTIFICATION/SOLUTION OF THE UFO PHENOMENA. DR ▓▓▓▓ FEELS THAT THE EFFORTS OF INDEPENDENT RESEARCHERS, ▓▓▓▓▓▓▓▓▓▓▓▓▓▓▓▓▓▓▓▓▓▓▓▓▓▓▓▓▓▓, ARE VITAL FOR FURTHER PROGRESS IN THIS AREA. AT THE PRESENT TIME, THERE ARE OFFICES AND PERSONNEL WITHIN THE AGENCY WHO ARE MONITORING THE UFO PHENOMENA, BUT AGAIN, THIS IS NOT CURRENTLY ON AN OFFICIAL BASIS. DR ▓▓▓▓ FEELS THAT THE BEST APPROACH WOULD BE TO KEEP IN TOUCH WITH AND IN FACT DEVELOP REPORTING CHANNELS IN THIS AREA TO KEEP THE AGENCY/COMMUNITY INFORMED OF ANY NEW DEVELOPMENTS. IN PARTICULAR, ANY INFORMATION WHICH MIGHT INDICATE A THREAT POTENTIAL WOULD BE OF INTEREST, AS WOULD SPECIFIC INDICATIONS OF FOREIGN DEVELOPMENTS OR APPLICATIONS OF UFO RELATED RESEARCH.

4. DR ▓▓▓▓ HAS ADVISED US THAT HE WOULD EVALUATE ANY ADDITIONAL INFORMATION WE MIGHT RECEIVE AS WELL AS DISSEMINATE SIGNIFICANT DEVELOPMENTS THROUGH APPROPRIATE CHANNELS SHOULD IT BE WARRANTED.

5. WE WISH TO STRESS AGAIN, THAT THERE DOES NOT NOW APPEAR TO BE ANY SPECIAL PROGRAM ON UFOS WITHIN THE INTELLIGENCE COMMUNITY AND THIS SHOULD BE RELAYED TO ▓▓▓▓▓▓

High strange is a term that has come to be associated with unexplainable sightings, specifically in relation to military, paranormal and UFO phenomena. Recorded incidents are allocated a strangeness rating and each witness is given a reliability rating. If an event has been designated both high strange and high reliable then a team of investigators are assigned.

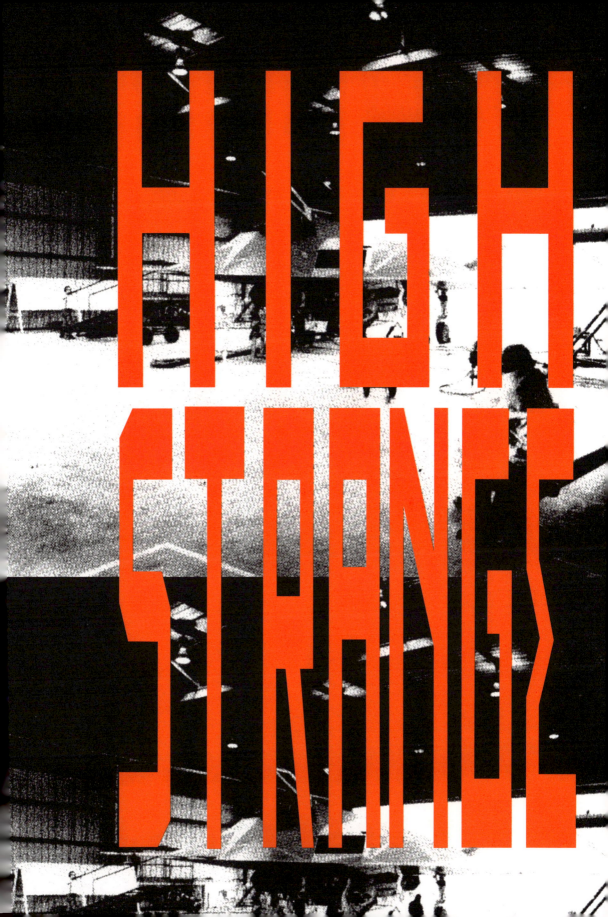

S. RADAR TRACKING O
FLYING OBJECTS [UFO
UFO [PROBABLY BALLO
THE AREA NEAR
———————— TOWARD WES
———————— AND ——————
———————— **ALT** 72,100
———————— TO UNIDENT
OBJECTS [UFO]: 0010
[PROBABLY BALLOONS]
BETWEEN
———————— AND ——————
———————— TOWARD WES
———————— AND ——————
———————— **ALT** 16,500

UNIDENTIFIED
0950-1210, EIGHT
ONS] MOVED FROM

AND FADED

88,580 FT. 6.
FIED FLYING
0910, 25 [UFO]
MOVED FROM AREA

AND PASSED

85,300 FT. OVER

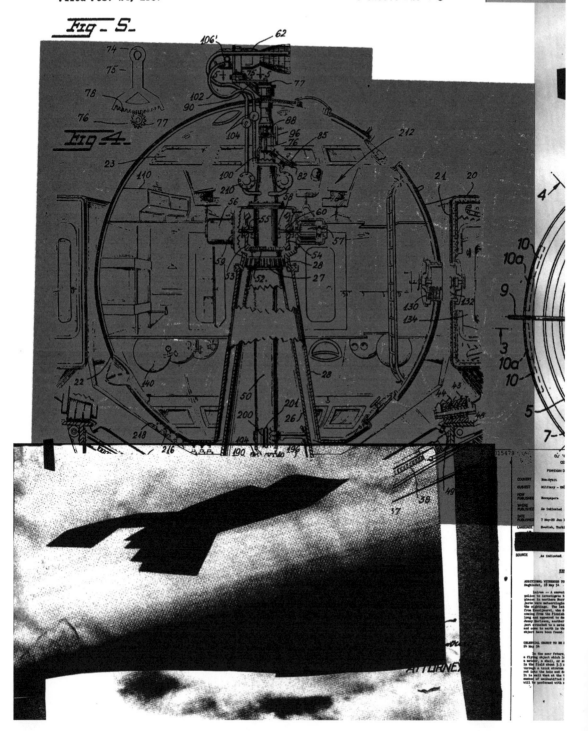

 ROUTINE

DAY 01

RECORD 01 A: On the Range

To describe the landscape as empty would be to give it too much character. It appears erased. Things seem to be missing. If it wasn't for our informant, waving us down by the side of the road we would have just kept driving. In the dust was a distant line of orange markers, banal survey sticks uncomfortably tipping as if from a forgotten building site that has long been left.

Across that boundary the resolution drops. It is an anomaly on the satellite image, a black site. This is where he wanted to meet us, where he said they keep the ▓▓▓▓▓.

'Across that boundary, no do overs, no second chances, they will detain you. We are all being filmed now so if you screw up they have evidence. Don't mess around, it will be an ugly weekend for you.'

We hadn't seen any cameras from the road. ▓▓▓▓▓▓▓▓ pointed to a telephone pole and switching box on a small hill just to the right of an unkempt service road. The dirt was still and undisturbed and it looked like no vehicle had used the road in a long time.

'Right now we are where we are allowed to be, but just beyond these signs is the boundary. If you take a look at on the hill there are these two remote cameras, one of them at least is pointing at us, and one of them is pointing down the road. Just up around the corner here is a guard shack where these guys can get out of the heat. That video and whatever else they got out here is transmitted to that shack. That's how they knew we were coming. They knew a long time before we got out here.'

What is known about the Range and its purpose has never formed a complete picture. A history of compartmentalised knowledge means that it is unclear if anyone has ever understood it as a whole. It exists to those outside its borders only in the stories that are told around it. The site is a series of fictions, whispered wilful misunderstandings and half-remembered anecdotes. A collection of carefully curated distant views, widely understood to be merely

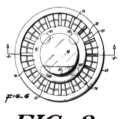

FIG. 2

elaborate visual illusions, mirages and decoys. A place constructed from mangled hearsay and untrustworthy eyes. It exists in the drunken tales told by old soaks propping up bars. In the whispered earnest insistences of embattled or embittered ex-employees of ███, of fantasists and opportunists who inhabit the perimeter of the Range, flocking like seagulls to landfill, picking off juicy bits of old news. We have come to listen, to circle the boundary and document its stories. On the Range there are two landscapes, one out there and one here, in the imagination, in memory.

RECORD 01 B: Dead Air

On our dash the GPS is still. It hasn't been updating since we entered the Range. No bars on the phones, it's a confronting silence. The soundtrack to this place is static. Black sites – white noise.

'They launched something from ~~White Sands~~, but it drifted off course and crashed. Since then the radio's been dead. Everyone around here knows you can't get a signal. We have to go into town if we want to talk to the world but not many people do. You have to be comfortable with the strangeness out here.'

RECORD 01 C: In the Still, Still Sky

Our bus lumbers up to a rocky lookout and the group gathers with a few of the border locals. We are told that it is here that most activity is spotted. In the absence of TV reception they spend many nights just sitting together to watch the sky. There is an old couch alone in the desert, a monument to the long nights that came before, stained with stories of strange sights and spilt beer. As the darkness creeps across the ground out comes the half-seen and the perceptually illusive.

'Out over the dry ~~desert~~ lake bed we saw a red light that looked like a laser pointer, pointing at a black chalkboard. It wasn't completely dark, just very nearly, a little bit of sunlight left and it hung out over there for the 15 or 20 minutes that we stood there. They were projecting some type

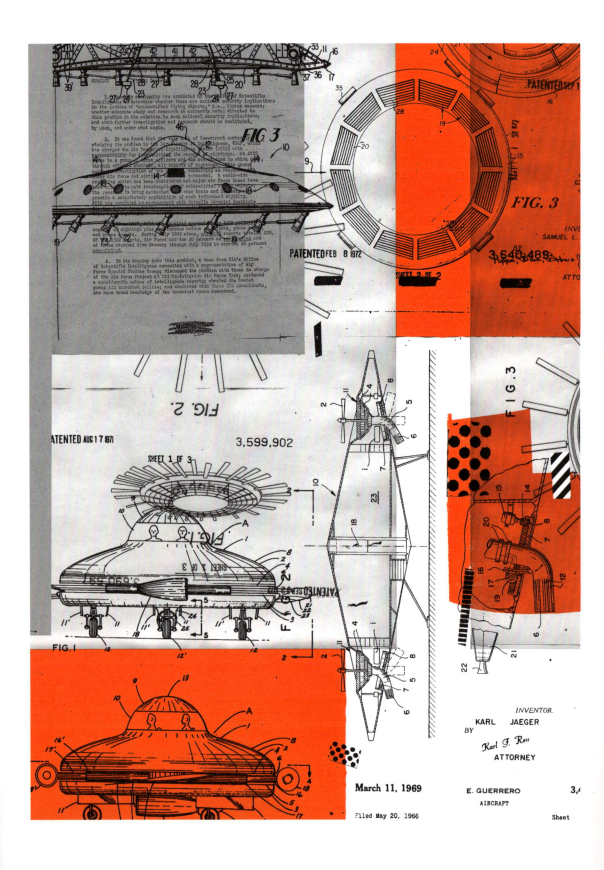

of laser for whatever reason but it wasn't hitting clouds as the sky was clear. I think it's some sort of remotely piloted drone that has anti-mag capabilities. There were no visible thrusters, there was no contrail, there was no indication at all of how that thing was being kept up in the air and how it was powered. I assume that our government has technology that is light years ahead of what ███████ admit publicly, but it's operational right now.

'Don't be surprised if strange things fly in the desert and yes, some of those are ours, and some of them do have some strange characteristics.

'I don't know if anyone in them can make the high G turns, let alone the survivability of a biological entity when you are up over Mach 9. You'd physically disintegrate unless you know how to manipulate time and space, and that I put well beyond our kinds of capability. Not something we could do without assistance anyway.

'They will make a right turn without any power, they go back and forth, or they come in and they go out, you'll see them and then you won't see them. You just have to keep looking up there. These are the things that ███████ are building out there, way beyond the black.'

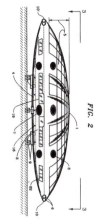

The sky is still … and empty.

DAY 02

RECORD 02 A: The Boneyard

Our bus pulled up to an old salvage yard. Parts of strange machines lay in the dirt like the skeletons of ancient dinosaurs. The sand was black with oil stains. At one point these decaying relics were the pinnacle of military technology, now they bake in the sun, preserved in the dry air of the desert. We meet ████, a mechanic who once worked across the line, and we ask him about where he used to work and what he used to build.

'I never met anyone that knew what ███████ was entirely, just people who were building pieces or components. That's the way they do it, you see? You are contracted to make just one piece of the puzzle, but no one knows exactly where it fits in the big plan. A thousand people, making harmless fragments. That's how you keep a secret, that's

how they made the F117 Stealth Nighthawk. They have just about retired that one so they would already be working on something to replace it. They gotta be designing something out there and I think they're in the design development phase right now but there's work going on, there's no two ways about it. It might be 10 years down the road before we know what's going on. If you are building something that is designed to be invisible, how can you ever see it?

'I read somewhere that our military technology advances 15 years for every one of our calendar years. We don't use anything in our daily life that the military hasn't already used.'

RECORD 02 B: Dr Death

The edges of the Range, near the boneyard, are home to a large number of ex-military men. It seems that they just don't want to leave. ████████ ████████████ was one of them, he wore a badge and authority emanated from him, at one time the military had given his ideas a lot of money. His website is a stream of photos; of him posing with this or that senior intelligence figure or with this or that Black-Ops scientist; of him diffusing bombs in Korea or Vietnam… And then there was the fact that he was a good friend of Uri Geller, and had spent a far amount of time getting high in the South American jungle.

'I was the director of advanced systems concepts so I was handling a lot of very, very high tech. All of the directed energy stuff, lasers, high-powered microwaves, particle beams, and all of that…precision-guided munitions, reconnaissance surveillance target acquisitions kind of thing. No one knew what the hell we were up to so I had a lot of flexibility and a lot of money. I was able to bring people in and this was how I created this ad-hoc study committee that went into the ████ in particular.'

'I ended up here, working part-time, with a private aerospace guy called ████████████. Instead of throwing up tin cans like the International Space Station what they do is inflatables. I think these explain most of the sightings out here but no one is going to tell you that. They lend themselves to different kinds of stories. I had stumbled into black programmes before and I knew what happened when you bumped into things you're not supposed to bump into.

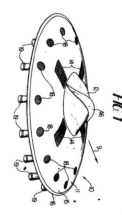

FIG. 1

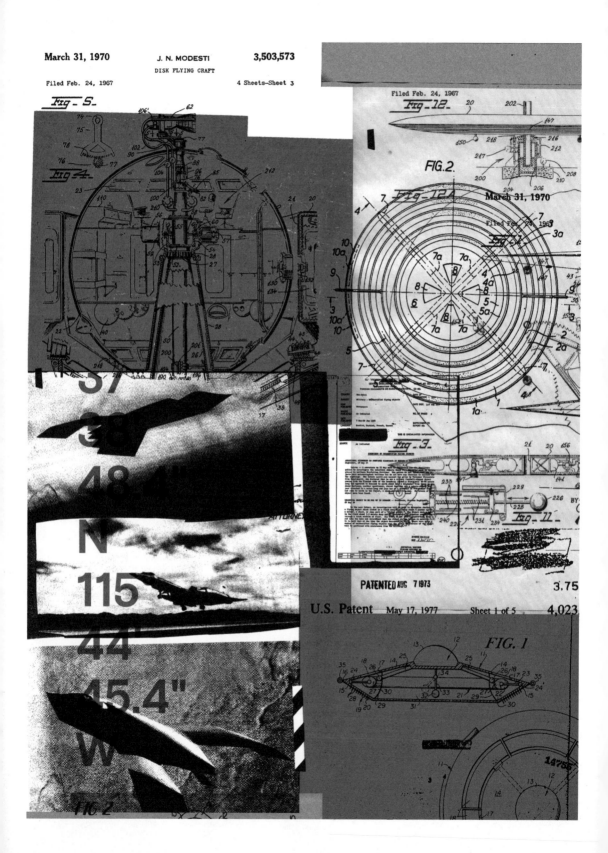

'Military people can't go public because of their security clearance and their own fear of losing their retirement and their safety and their families' safety. We won't know about it until they have completely investigated it and have the military advantage over it.'

RECORD 02 C: Sentinels

The territory beyond the border was charged with something invisible, poured out on the dirt in front of us. This was a myth made ground. The white SUV parked on the crest of a hill a few hundred feet away had the word sentinel painted on its side. That was all that was needed to fundamentally alter our relationship to this small patch of otherwise unremarkable scrubland. The imagination is sent wild by this kind of sign, and the thrill of conspiracy sparks in the dry desert air.

'He said 'you'll know it if you see it,' and here in the air is something the size of an aircraft carrier, and this thing had been there hovering around and we had it on radar and they go to fire on it and this thing takes off and in two sweeps in about two seconds this thing had transited about 250 miles. This is the early 1950s. No we don't have anything that can go from zero to thousands of miles per hour. Some of them are obviously advanced technology. Part of the problem is that the sceptical explanation is sometimes more unbelievable than the actual events that may have happened.'

DAY 03

RECORD 03 A: Neon Ruin

The motel we were directed to had long been abandoned and would be a good place to shelter from the wind. Lovers had scrawled their names in the concrete, the hieroglyphs of college road trips and conspiracy tourists. In the neon ruin, ▮▮▮ told us of the nights he used to spend in the bar here. It was the only place to drink on the Range and tonight it will hear stories again. His stories were the sort you only heard in bars, and what he knew about the ▮▮▮▮▮▮▮ was whiskey-soaked.

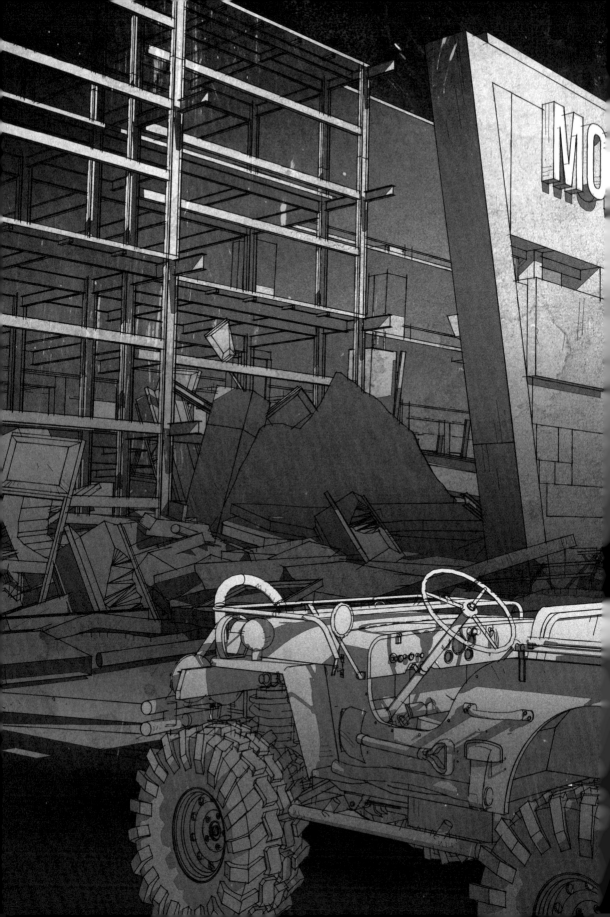

'One morning, while I was having breakfast here, I met ▮▮▮ who had a really nice notebook. It was beautiful, almost calligraphy handwriting. He said let me ask you something and I said "sure go ahead" and, you know, I was a little bit drunk and he said "have you seen one of these". He had a page with all this writing and above it was a gorgeous, artistic profile of a ▮▮▮. I said no but he said he had seen it last night on the hill.

'I don't know if any of you were out speaking to him last night but he was telling us a story that back in the 70s he flew a ▮▮▮. He was dead serious, he's a smart guy but maybe he'd had a few too many Jim Beams. ▮▮▮▮▮▮ asked if it was hard to fly and he said no, it's a mind integration something or other, I mean he had this elaborate term and I just couldn't stand it anymore. You don't know what to believe besides your own eyes and I don't even believe them sometimes.'

We were standing in what was once the gift shop. There was an economy to these tales. Inflatable green men lie crumpled under the rubble, a 'truth is out there' coffee mug fractured on the floor. This is how this landscape spreads. It is an atomised territory that has long left its physical borders behind. It sits on the shelf of a study, in a box in the attic, on a guitar case or school bag. We peel a bumper sticker off the wall for our bus — My Other Car is a Spaceship.

RECORD 03 B: Myth-Maker

We were up on a rocky outcrop, about three miles from the line. We'd climbed in the heat to get a view out over the east side of the zone while the sun was setting and the ▮▮▮▮▮▮ were visible. ▮▮▮▮ was the professional folklorist. It seemed not even he believed everything he said, but he made a pretty good living out of telling tall tales to people out in this landscape. ▮▮▮▮▮▮ is a new age magnet, its alleged force fields and cosmic lay lines have attracted a steady stream of kooks and charlatans since the 60s. Here, perpetuating a myth is a business plan. We could see shadows of a vast structure about five miles from the outcrop we were standing on.

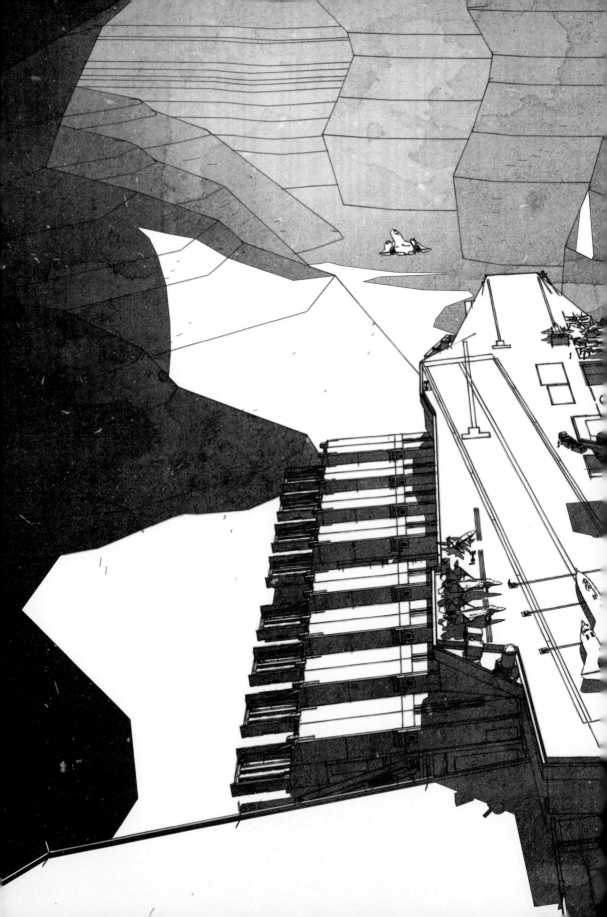

'Look at how far humans have progressed with technology in the last 300 years, even in the last 60 years. How long were dinosaurs around, maybe 300 million years? How do we know that in the last million years dinosaurs didn't evolve and become sentient and space-faring and they knew an asteroid was coming and they left, or they moved underground to save themselves, and now all these evil reptoids are actually evolved dinosaurs reclaiming earth from us primates. It makes more sense to me than some reptoids coming all the way from 'Draconius' to rape jazz singers in LA. They are back checking up on the experiment, not sure we did very well, but you know. If little grey guys from Zeta Reticuli are dropping in, you know we must be on the start map for the bucket list.'

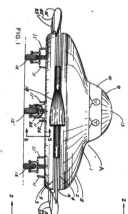

Day 04

RECORD 04 A: What Lies Beneath

```
A grainy photo showed the relic of what must
have been an old mining machine — too heavy and
cumbersome to have ever flown — piles of tailings
marked the flat ground like a constellation of
pyramids. In the back room of the military museum
in ▓▓▓▓▓▓▓▓ — a short man, who sounded like a
preacher, and looked like a university lecturer
— was flicking earnestly through slides on a
powerpoint. It seemed an oddly banal medium to
convey his message.
```

'We were out there digging tunnels for the project. Our facility was mostly underground, you know there is a network of tunnels that run all through here and connect back to ▓▓▓▓▓▓▓. That's how they get in or out without anybody seeing them. One of my buddies was working and he happened to spot what looked like stains coming down from a hole in the rock face so at risk of life and limb he went up there and claims that he found a vast underground city, filled with 33 mummies, a wide variety of Asian and what he thought were Egyptian-style artefacts, including what looked like very impressive gold Buddha. He immediately reported this to the ▓▓▓▓▓▓▓▓ and they sent out an archaeologist to document the find just like you guys are doing now. According to some rumours they pulled out 109 truckloads of artefacts, completely mapped the underground city and

then totally went into denial and said that they didn't find anything and that it was all just a big misunderstanding. I think that is why this is all here. Maybe this is where all the technology comes from. You can't see it, but there is something special about this place.'

RECORD 04 B: It and They

We were skirting the black zone, circling a heavy nothingness where all roads were punctuated by dead ends and no-go destinations. We stood on hard soil, sun flare in cheap sunglasses, staring at a sign that asked us less than politely not to go any further. There are few road signs out here; we get where we are going because ▓▓▓ has drawn a map on the windscreen with a marker pen. We guess people out here know where they are going. People out here also know exactly where they are not going. Where we were not going was past the sign. We could see evidence of people, of workers, but there was no movement. In the hot sun, the silence felt like a brooding and perpetual siesta.

'This is the gate where they bring in workers via a bus, normal maintenance traffic comes in here, 18-wheelers hauling who knows what and big cargo carriers come in here to go to the base. We saw weird shit happen that you cannot believe, I mean REALLY REALLY strange that absolutely happened. I've always maintained that 'IT', whatever 'IT' is, is in charge, it is sentient, it knows what you're going to do. I have no idea where they're from, I really don't. I don't believe it's from our solar system, I think it's further out and I don't think time travel would be a problem.'

'Threats are real, they do threaten you. They will change your name, they will change your location. There is no limit to what ▓▓▓▓▓▓▓▓▓▓ will do to keep this story quiet. That secrecy tends to get people to fill in the blanks with very active imaginations.'

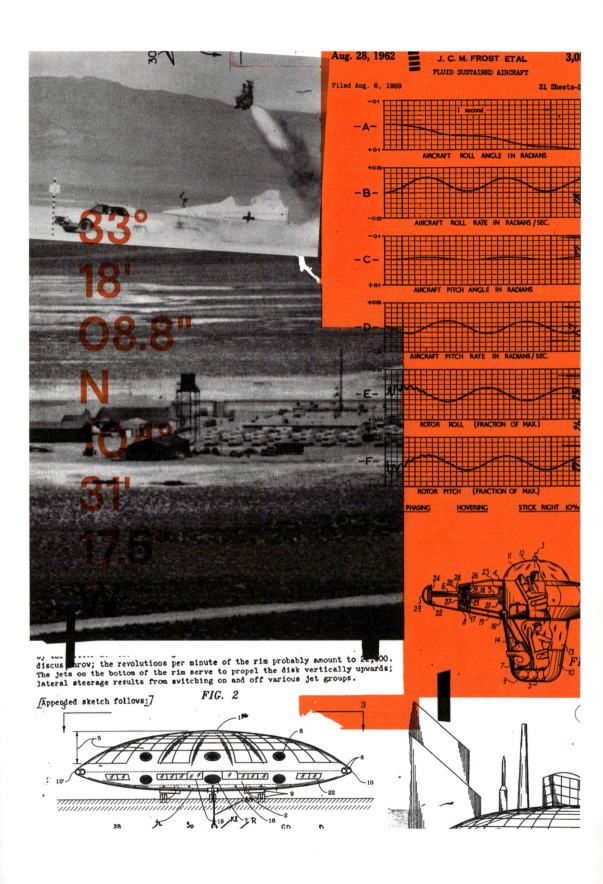

Day 05

RECORD 05 A: Nowhere & Everywhere

We stood by a 7ft wire fence, outside a hangar in ▆▆▆▆▆▆. A town that holds an annual ▆▆▆ nut-job convention, and whose Walmart is adorned with little green men and a flying saucer is filling up at the gas station on the high street. It was a shitty town, a run-down place, where the alien theme smacked you in the face everywhere you looked. 'Alien parking', 'Alien Coca-Cola' vending machines — a museum with diorama 'reconstructions' of extra-terrestrial visitations. The only viable business, it seemed, was selling t-shirts and other alien-shaped or stamped crap out of shabby looking storefronts. In a place that was a parody of itself, a joke town, with bumper-sticker humour, ▆▆▆▆▆ was a diehard believer, a former engineer, sincere and likeable in a Stetson and western shirt. He had spent a good chunk of his life in pursuit of the truth, travelling all over the country chasing leads. He'd got himself involved with some disinformation tactics of the US government and he'd been told a lot of things by a lot of people. ▆▆▆▆▆ was pinning his hopes on the deathbed confessions of the last living witnesses to the incident. The empty hangar was now owned by a courier company. Around it was nondescript light industry. We were nowhere and everywhere.

'I think obtaining the truth is so important that I have dedicated my life to it. Unfortunately most people believe what is on the internet. I don't know who would admit after 60 years that they lied. I don't see that happening. If you see a ▆▆▆ or if you have some form of experience then it is something that you just don't forget. That's something that has been consistent with all the people I have talked to. There is never anybody that has a doubt about what they saw. The problem we have is proving it.

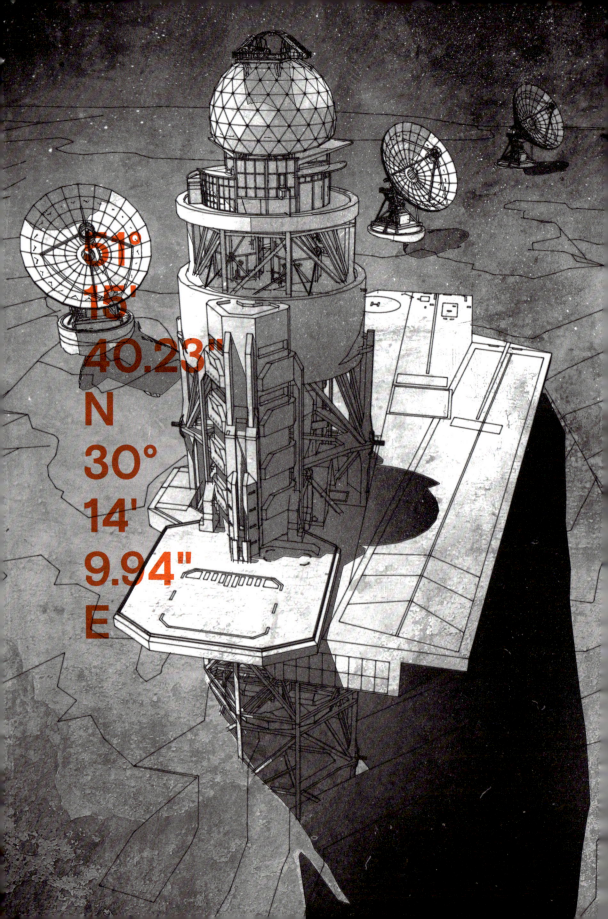

CENTRAL INTELLIGENCE AGENCY
INFORMATION FROM
FOREIGN DOCUMENTS OR RADIO BROADCASTS

REPORT NO. 00-W-23602
CD NO. --
DATE OF INFORMATION 1952
DATE DIST. 16 Aug 1952
NO. OF PAGES 2

'This is probably one of the biggest buildings related to the ▓▓▓▓ and I am really hoping that this stays preserved because if this story turns out to be true, which many of us think it is, then this building could turn out to be the building of the millennium.'

RECORD 05 A: War People

▓▓▓▓ was a tall and wiry, his was a true , southwest drawl, his face was spectacular, one you found yourself staring into, traversing its pocks and crevasses as he talked — as much landscape as the dry hills that surrounded us. We were standing in his yard, revolvers in hand, sights on a line of cans perched on a fence post. Bang. Each story was bookended by the crack of a bullet missing a tin can.

'It was dark, they saw a bright light in the forest, and Travis made the mistake of getting out of the truck, walking over to it and the light just zapped him up into the craft. 5 days later he came down, 30 miles away. He is one of the few abductees I can put a lot of confidence in and believe because you can look in the man's face and know that he experienced something very unusual.'

Another man wandered out to join us. A dog barked from behind the fly-screened back door as it flapped shut behind him. He launched straight in without introductions, he knew what the topic would be without needing to ask.

'We were talking last night that if you stop and think that even given all the technology that we have had in the last 50 years we still can't go out there. If they can come here then their technology and knowledge must be so far advanced, maybe 100, a 1,000 or 1,0000 years ahead of us. We can't even imagine what their technology might be. My thinking is that they're watching us.

'To be honest with you I am scared for our country and for our world because of the way things are happening. We are a war people, we are the only species that can't get along with each other. Why would they want to communicate with us unless they are watching to make sure we don't self-destruct.'

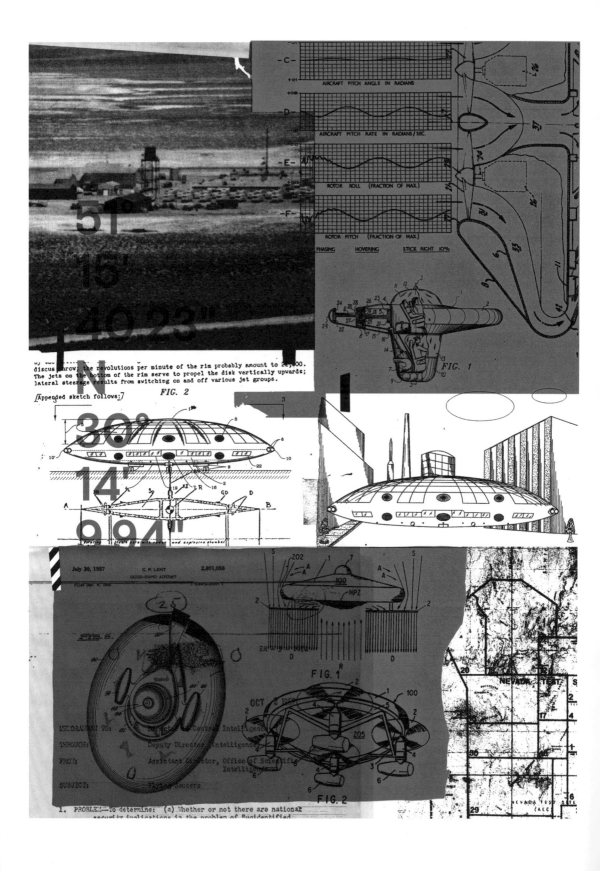

Day 06

RECORD 06 A: Voodoo Warriors of the Pentagon

The southern road out to the ▓▓▓▓ border is a road that imposes an epic vanishing point on the landscape in the manner of a road going somewhere, with little of interest to it along the way. A directness. Sharp lines of movement vanish at the horizon in landscapes like this before they have the chance to be hidden, because there is nothing to hide them. All that is visible is laid bare, that's what makes the place so beguiling. From the ground you can see clear into it across a barren landscape dotted with structures that defy interpretation.

Secrecy laces hearsay into the land, obscuring meaning and disrupting the logic of rational conclusions. These are naked territories punctuated by all manner of cloaking. The territory's most effective strategy was the way it disrupted confidence in the rules, in the foundations of belief. How could one construct in one's mind in a coherent picture of what was being constructed on this site, if even the laws of physics were in doubt?

'There are physical things that transit our physical universe, 95% have prosaic answers, but there resides a residual amount that just defy all explanation. Whatever this is it's more complex than we have ever imagined. I argue that we are not even asking the right questions yet, never mind even getting close to having any hard answers.

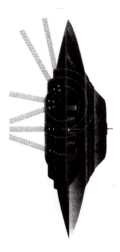

'Among the strange things I did in the ▓▓▓▓▓▓▓▓ is work with psychokinesis. Yes it really does work and sometimes you get some pretty spectacular results. They wrote an article called 'The Voodoo Warriors of the Pentagon', which was us. From there I ended up getting invited into the intelligence community to look at these areas. I was briefing a 3 star who was the head of one of our letters intelligence agencies, telling us about what he saw. Here's a guy who's a head of an agency, who's seen ▓▓▓▓ and is really sure it wasn't an optical illusion or atmospheric phenomena or anything like that.'

RECORD 06 B: The Quiet Professionals

We sat in a car park just outside ▮▮▮▮▮▮ city limits, We had arranged to meet ▮▮▮▮, unknowingly under a busy flight path into ▮▮▮▮▮▮ airport. And his hushed revelations were periodically drowned out by the sound of low-flying aircraft, adding a conspiratorial air to each sentence.

'Who are the 'quiet professionals'? That's US Special Operations Command. The guys with green berets. We sit back and think big thoughts.'

The currency of belief was a very serious one. ▮▮▮▮▮▮▮▮▮▮▮▮▮▮ and his colleagues at the ▮▮▮▮ could not be blindsided by technology they didn't believe in.

'I take on both the true believers who are gullible and would believe anything and the sceptics who are really debunkers and the basic problem is a fundamental belief system. We could have a ▮▮▮▮▮▮▮ hovering above us right now and we wouldn't see it. A number of people see things and just disregard it; it can't be, therefore it isn't. But we also know sometimes you just don't see them because you have no context. And there are things that are just flat overwhelming. The human mind is limited, I can't imagine a universe that doesn't stop but just keeps going. Everything we know is point A to point B. but it just keeps going and I can't comprehend that really.

'What is accepted as fact changes over time, and this comes back to belief systems, ok, what facts am I willing to accept as evidence, what's my standard of proof? Most of the phenomena we are discussing and ▮▮▮▮ in particular, if you take human perception out of it, you still end up with things that are indefinable, that just do not make sense.

'Just because you get information that you don't understand doesn't mean you should a-priori reject it. The downside to secrecy is lack of support, as well as people filling in the blanks and creating wild stories and things.'

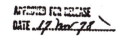

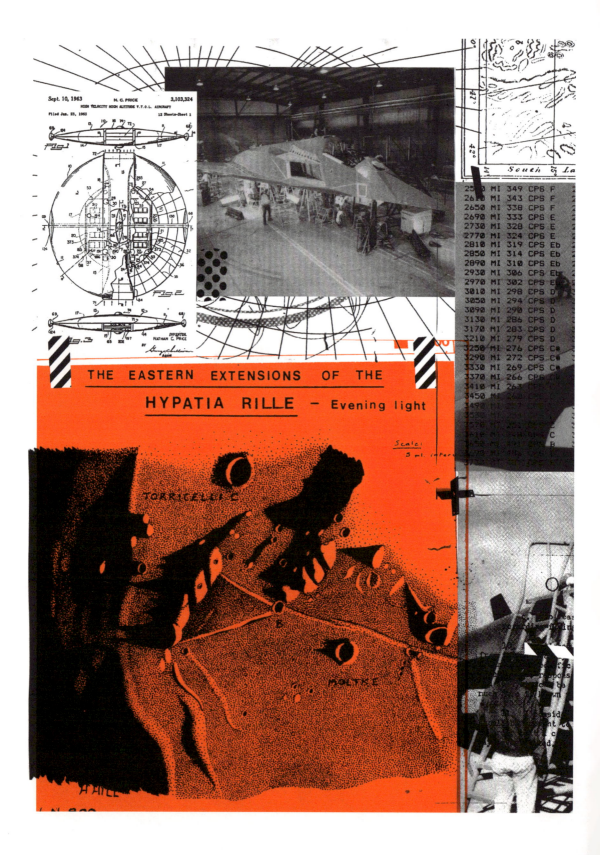

Day 07: FINAL DAY ON THE RANGE

RECORD 07 A: Fiction Machines

For all its emptiness it still draws people close. This is a landscape for the projection of belief and disbelief, of wonder and of fear. We had one last person to meet: ▮▮▮▮. He boasted about his security clearance, he was as high up as they come, as close to the centre as we could get. And his job? Storyteller. Travelling state to state. Feeding tales into the collective consciousness.

The real product of this site? Not some experimental fighter, or a frozen alien corpse but the simple possibility that it could be all of these and none of them. That ambiguity is more potent than anything else that could have been developed. The 'machine' they were all building was a ghost, a set of incoherent fragments designed to produce stories. They believed each component was part of a whole. But it wasn't. They weren't building a machine, they were the machine, one with no other purpose than the manufacture of fiction. These stories won the Cold War. This is the weapon ultimately launched from this site.

'It was my job to tell them. At every convention of kooks and crackpots, at every bar I could find I would sing my song. We fill in the blank spots on the map with our own imaginations.'

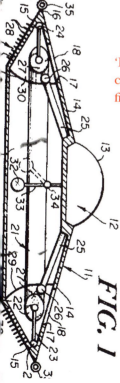

FIG. 1

The machines of war wield their power through knowledge. The power resides with those who know, and those who remain in the dark are disempowered and left to construct a cloud of their own meaning around an unobtainable truth. In this landscape truth was not important, in its place was a self-perpetuating machine for confusion. Too many stories woven into the fabric of collective consciousness to erase now. These black sites have always manufactured something potent. Because whatever materialised physically within their bounds — and what that was we may never know he true product of this place was what reached beyond these shadows.

The landscapes manufactured something immaterial. They were story factories, instruments of weaponised folklore. Notions of confidence, security and national pride, of fear, threat, bluff and deception were all forged in the foundry of fictions that lay beyond those charged fences. This landscape was the hidden poker hand of the Cold War; the magician's sleeve, where territory had become the assembly line of myth creation. A purposeful void, to be filled by productive speculation, where the story was the weapon itself.

THE STORY IS THE WEAPON

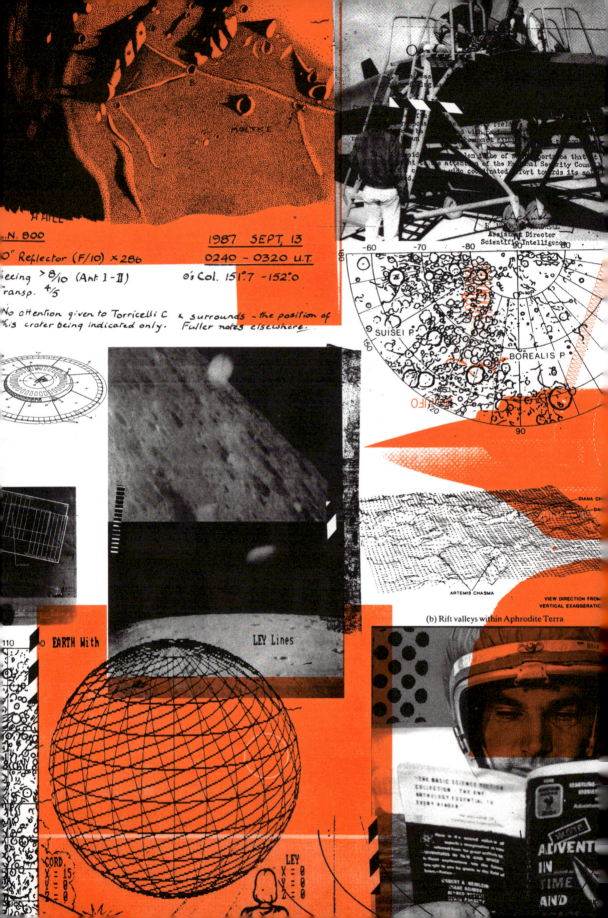